Poland
A Pilgrim's Companion

by
David Baldwin

Dedicated to Saint Maximilian Kolbe,
who offered the ultimate sacrifice of love,
in laying down 'his life for his friends'. (*Jn* 15:13)

*All booklets are published thanks to the
generous support of the members of the
Catholic Truth Society*

CATHOLIC TRUTH SOCIETY
PUBLISHERS TO THE HOLY SEE

Contents

Why Poland? 3

Kraków and the Royal Cathedral 12

The Old Town of Kraków 26

Sanctuary of the Divine Mercy 34

Nowa Huta and the Salt Mines 45

Kalwaria Sanctuary and Wadowice 56

Our Lady of Częstochowa 66

Auschwitz 77

Mercy and Reconciliation 97

With grateful thanks for advice and feedback to Sr Gabriela Gasz COLW, Henry Gierszewski and Ernest Mirolsav of Ernesto Travel.

Why Poland?

On the face of it Poland may not be the most obvious place to venture on a major pilgrim journey. I went with only rather hazy expectations and a general sense of curiosity. Yet this was the place from which Pope John Paul II hailed - preceded by modern saints about whom I knew a little, and instinctively admired - St Faustina, associated with the Divine Mercy, and St Maximilian Kolbe, martyred at Auschwitz. Little did I know the wider treasures that awaited me, which gave such surprise and inspiration as my journey unfolded. This small book is your invitation to have a look at the Poland that I discovered through pilgrim eyes, and for you to examine the case for going there - so that at least you can have some facts, and a 'taster', before deciding.

This is not a guide book in the conventional sense. It will reinforce any other regular guides you may use on your travels; it may point out aspects not covered elsewhere. At some venues it may be all that you have in English - not all the Polish sites are geared extensively for the English speaking visitors - which ironically, is part of the charm of these places. This book necessarily concentrates on the pilgrim aspect of your visit, and as such, includes accompanying meditations and prayers. There are, of course, many other attractions that may, quite rightly, also catch your attention.

A Catholic country

Apart from being an attractive 'European style' country to which you can relate, it is still very much a Catholic country, with a largely devout and faithful population. Of course, the incursion of modern Western life is beginning to have an impact since Poland joined the EU, but it is still a place where Christianity is an important ingredient of daily life. This is generally very much in evidence with the abundance of active churches, the struggle to keep Sunday special, the frequency and importance given to Adoration of the Blessed Sacrament, and the bulging seminaries - the priests all look so young!

The high and intense level of Marian devotion also struck me. Major devotions and intercessory prayer are centred round Our Lady, usually through the 'windows' of prominent holy icons. Many churches throughout the land are dedicated to her - as will become evident as you follow this book.

Variety of pilgrim destinations

With that as background, Poland also offers some significant, specific pilgrim destinations, linked with events and people, that lend a dimension of international interest. They are of relevance to our world, and have, and will continue to have, a bearing on our own Christian lives.

Most of these pilgrim places are conveniently centred in and around Kraków - itself a very attractive city in the broadest sense - and of which the pilgrim element is explored in detail in ensuing Chapters. Like it or not, cut price airlines offer cheap and accessible entry for the independent pilgrim.

In Kraków itself, there is the beautiful, eccentric Royal Cathedral, an impressive Basilica to Our Lady, and a host of interesting churches and places within easy reach. All portray different aspects of Catholic life through the history of the Church and of Poland. In the southern suburbs, at Łagiewniki, is the striking, huge, brand-new Basilica of the Divine Mercy, where Saint Faustina's mortal remains rest, and from where the inspirational devotion to the Divine Mercy has spread world-wide.

In the north eastern suburbs there is the vast 'new town' of Nowa Huta, a communist inspired social development. Here there are some extraordinary churches - some old - but others built with blood, grinding toil and dedication during the communist regime, including the most remarkable Ark of Our Lord, the Arka Pana. Not far outside Kraków are the extensive underground Salt Mines at Wieliczka, where you will see within the underground mine workings an exquisite, sizeable chapel carved entirely from salt. Also within an easy bus ride to the west, is the heavily fortified 11th century Benedictine Abbey of Tyniec, dominating the River Wisła, below.

Further afield, a short, linking train-ride on the smart, modern 'papal train' from Kraków, will take you to the extensive, rurally placed Stations of the Cross with its Baroque Franciscan Basilica at Kalwaria, and then on to the small, charming town of Wadowice, Pope John Paul II's birthplace. Not far to the north west of Kraków is the town of Częstochowa, over which the fortress monastery of the Pauline monks of Jasna Góra looms, housing the miraculous icon of the Black Madonna - the spiritual heart of Poland. And then there is Auschwitz - that grim testament to man's limitless inhumanity to his fellow man - that needs to be visited, and prayed at, as a salutary and sobering reminder.

People

Then there are the people that constantly weave in and out of this tapestry: Pope John Paul II, Saint Faustina, Saint Maximilian Kolbe, Saint Teresa Benedicta of the Cross (Edith Stein) - all known to us as Catholics, all having an impact on our lives somewhere along the line. There is also the heroic Father Jerzy Popiełuszko of Warsaw, possibly not so well known, murdered by the communist regime in 1984.

Geography

Poland is situated at the southern end of the Baltic Sea, surrounded by Germany to the west, the Czech Republic and Slovakia to the south, Ukraine and Belarus to the east, with Lithuania and the Russian enclave of Kaliningrad to the north. In area it is a fifth again larger than the United Kingdom, with a population of 38.5 million people centred mainly on cities and medium sized towns, and of which 90% is Catholic. Inland, it has a temperate continental climate with warm summers and cold winters - winter being drier than summer!

A turbulent history

Surprisingly little detail is known about Poland's history before 966 - most of it having to rely on rather scant archaeological finds rather than any record or human testament. Archaeology has shown signs of people living there in the Stone, Bronze and Iron Ages, but of uncertain ethnicity, thought to be Germanic, Celtic and Baltic tribes.

What is known, is of a turbulent, fractured, ever-changing place. At its most powerful, it had huge territories and close alliances reaching wide into Ukraine, Russia and the Baltics; at its lowest, it existed in ideal only, with its neighbours on two occasions having attempted to wipe it off the map. Yet despite this, a unique Polish culture and ethnicity have survived and developed throughout the centuries, and this is very evident today.

Christianity

It was only in the middle of the tenth century that, from past obscurity, emerged a recognisable single, territorial entity with the institution of a monarchy which coincided with the arrival of Christianity in the region. The first king was baptised in 966 and Christianity proclaimed as the 'official religion'. Strangely, it is reported that Christianity initially came in the form of a Slavonic mission of the Greek Oriental Church. However, the close connection at the time with Germany, through treaty and marriage, gradually brought ascendancy of the Roman Church, and in 968 the first Polish bishopric was established in Poznań.

In the first centuries of its existence the nation was led by a series of strong monarchical rulers, integrating this raw, young country into European culture. But by nature of its geographical and strategic location there were also many periods of complicated turbulence, with fragmentation, reunification and partition ebbing and flowing throughout the times. The 16th century saw a strong association with Lithuania, of which there is much evidence, even today. There was also a strong migration of Jews into the area, Poland being a tolerant and protective society to all migrants.

World Wars

The outcome of World War I destroyed the might of Germany and Russia, and allowed Poland to shake off these two predators on her borders. Poland was formally reconstituted and recognised as a unified state. World War II spelt a major disaster for Poland; the predators returned: it was split into two occupied zones - Soviet and German. A government in exile was established in London. Of the countries involved in the War, Poland lost the highest percentage of its citizens: over six million perished, half of them Polish Jews. Probably quite unknown, Poland made one of the largest troop contributions to the Allied war effort.

After the War the Communists instituted their totalitarian regime, in which democracy and Christianity were stifled. Many opposition leaders, including priests and religious were persecuted, jailed, and some murdered. Eventually, through the pressure of the workers' movement, Solidarity, encouraged by Pope John Paul II, the Communist monolith started to collapse, leading to the return of democracy, and membership of the EU in 2004.

Practical thoughts

A few practical thoughts. If you are a solo or independent pilgrim, recourse to some practical guide, such as the *Rough Guide*, would be very useful to help you plan your travel in detail. Getting around is relatively cheap and easy, maybe a bit slow at times, but there is a reasonably well developed infrastructure for car, train or bus. Poland is not a place for vegetarians or weight watchers! Poles seem to be hearty eaters, and meat, particularly pork, seems to be a vital part of the diet!

English is not widely spoken, certainly outside cities. If in doubt, single out young people; either that, or lots of pointing at maps and words - you will always find eager helpers! If, on visiting a church, you find you are struggling with access or information, it is always worth, as with many continental churches, in heading confidently for the Sacristy, which generally seems to be more available as a centre of help and information than our more remote sacristies. Seek out the Sister - usually bustling around somewhere - and although she may not speak a great deal of English, she may be willing to help you in your quest.

Mercy and Reconciliation

One of the specific reasons I personally went on pilgrimage to Poland was to somehow discover how (if?) one could reconcile the unspeakable horrors perpetrated at Auschwitz, and the concept - the actuality - of God's infinite Mercy, as propagated from the Divine Mercy Shrine just a short journey away in Kraków. I sensed a strong incongruous tension here. An entirely providential meeting with a Polish priest gave me just such evidence of God's Mercy. I believe I discovered this connection, and summarise this in the last Chapter - Mercy and Reconciliation - a theme you may wish to explore.

But you may, initially anyway, want to set a broader course, and just enjoy the variety and fascination that this country and its Faith offers. You may choose, as Pope Benedict did in his visit in May 2006, "to inhale this atmosphere of faith in which you live…to draw from the abundant fountain of your faith, which has flowed continuously for over a millennium, and I am confident that my pilgrimage during these days will encourage the faith that we share, both yours and mine".

Whatever course you take, it is a place from which you will return strengthened, enlightened and encouraged. I do commend it to you.

Kraków and the Royal Cathedral

Kraków

Kraków is located well to the south of Poland, a small city in quite an isolated rural setting, some 70 kms north of the border with Slovakia, and within sight of the scenic Tatra mountains. It is one of the oldest cities in Poland, and with Polish kings and queens having taken residence there for many hundreds of years, lays claim to being the ancient capital of Poland. And because of this, and its Cathedral being their coronation and final resting place - alongside artists, poets, national heroes and statesmen and women - it is also described as the heart and soul of the Polish nation. With the arrival of formal Christianity in Poland in the late 10th century, the Kraków See was established soon after, and the first cathedral was built on the present site in about 1020. The city abounds with churches - there are 414 parishes in the Kraków diocese, many of them being in and around the city!

It has been described as the 'most Italianate' of the northern cities because of the influence of celebrated Italian Renaissance architects brought here at the behest of Poland's sixteenth century rulers. But there is also evidence, through churches and other buildings, of the Middle Ages, Gothic and Baroque influences.

In more modern times the city suffered occupation by the Nazis during the Second World War and the Communist regime thereafter. Both had lasting effects on the city. With Kraków being a seat of government for the Nazi regime, the city, ironically, did not suffer any physical war damage; however, part of its unique character was destroyed with the elimination of the quite sizeable Jewish population, who were sent to nearby Auschwitz (see p. 77), and from which it never recovered. With the advent of communism, came the effort by that regime to redress the social mix in the Kraków area with the building of a huge steelworks and supporting suburbs of Nowa Huta (see p. 45).

Thankfully these modern suburbs are far enough away not to have directly affected Old Kraków's mediaeval charm. It is an attractive and compact city, with its hilltop castle and Cathedral complex, and with what claims to be the largest surviving market square of mediaeval Europe (Rynek Główny) in the picturesque Old Town (Stare Miasto). A lush green, tree-lined park (Planty) virtually encircles the Old Town, and the River Wisła flows lazily through the city. The Old Town is easily walkable, with plenty of spiritual and material 'pit stops' along any route. The entire city and suburbs are easily accessible with the efficient tram and bus system, at very reasonable cost, for those who want to wander at will further afield.

It is a popular holiday and tourist destination, but certainly in a pilgrim context this did not overly impinge. It is a pleasant, well organised, jolly place, very laid back and seemingly at ease with itself.

Wawel Hill

Wawel Hill is the geographic feature that dominates the river Wisła below and the surrounding town - the perfect place to locate a secure habitation. There is certainly evidence of early BC settlement here; of the pagan Vistulans between 7th and 11th centuries, and the establishment, in the early Middle Ages, of the castle and cathedral complex atop the hill as the residence for the monarchs. The whole complex has an authentic mediaeval feel to it. The walls and fortifications still stand solid, and the warm, red-brick buildings possessively encircle the sizeable green in the middle. It is a very pleasant place to visit - in or outside - offering lovely views, with cafés in which to refresh and relax. There is plenty to explore round here in the Castle and Museums, but under the constraints of my pilgrim brief, I must restrict our exploration to the Cathedral.

The Royal Cathedral, Kraków

The Royal Cathedral

There is little left of the first cathedral to give any accurate indication of how it looked, or what size it was. The second cathedral, was built between 1090 and 1142 in the Romanesque style. Some surviving elements of this building, damaged by fire in 1305 and general dilapidation, are shown by St Leonard's crypt and the lower section of the south tower. The third, current cathedral, is essentially Gothic, built between 1320 and 1364, and consecrated in March 1364. The Renaissance subsequently saw much development of the interior in that style; and with continuing generous endowments, the 'modernisation' continued on into the 17th and 18th centuries, particularly with the advent of Baroque.

All but four of the forty five monarchs of Poland are buried here, and with all these royal tombs, chapels, mausoleums and monuments, the whole gives a dazzling compendium of six centuries of Central European architecture, art, sculpture, Polish and Church history. This is all summed up beautifully - in terms of the cathedral's combined spiritual and architectural heritage - by the then Archbishop of Kraków, Karol Wojtyła, latterly Pope John Paul II: "The sanctuary of the nation…cannot be entered without an inner trembling, without an awe, for here - as in few cathedrals of the world - is contained a vast greatness which speaks to us of the history of Poland, of all our past."

First impressions

With all this crossing your mind, your first sight of the Cathedral as you look across the green from the southern entrance to the Wawel might just stop you in your tracks. Because what you see before you is a dizzying and compact mix of domes, towers, spires, cupolas; of copper, gold, red brick, pale stone - and this gives you the first clue as to what lies within - a huge amount of detail that comes at you thick and fast and in very short order! You will need time to attune to what is in this, actually quite small, building complex. There could be a danger of sensory overload, so take it easy - it is a challenge, but also a huge treat!

On the back of your entry ticket is shown a route of travel, and with the excellent official guide book, should be sufficient to take you round and tell and show you all you need or want to know. It is a 'working' cathedral, so some areas may be curtailed at various times as liturgical celebrations take place. These are some of the highlights of my wanderings, highly selective - no doubt you will have your own favourites, as well. Many of the side chapels, confusingly, have differing names or attributions - I have generally used the principal English name in the official guide book.

Once inside

On entering, yes, one is struck by the cathedral's relatively small size. The central nave is short, pillared, and seemingly foreshortened by what you see immediately in front of you - a magnificent black pillared, arched and gold-domed *baldacchino*. This splendid edifice is the canopy for the Reliquary of St Stanisław, the patron Saint of Poland, who was murdered at his altar by King Bolesław II in May 1079, in shades of Thomas Becket's murder, some decades later by Henry II. The elaborate Reliquary is of silver, in the form of a coffin, supported by four angels, and atop, his bishop's accoutrements held aloft by two cherubs. The votive candle was presented by Pope John Paul II when he celebrated Mass in 1979 at the cathedral on the 900th anniversary of Stanisław' martyrdom.

You will then thread right-handed past the *baldacchino* into what the guide book describes as the 'presbytery' but may in our terms, be the choir and sanctuary. Here is a veritable feast of colour, texture, shape and substance. The plain, vaulted roof, the large hanging wall tapestries, slender, tall, plain glass windows at the higher level, warm red brick walling contrasting with the wide, pointed Gothic arches at the lower level; then the deep dark wood of the intricately carved choir stalls, all lit from above by bright crystal or gilded chandeliers. The High Altar is extravagantly carved and gilded in the Baroque style, and the Tabernacle is topped by delicate gold pillars supporting an open, gold half-dome. I could not help but notice the Archbishop's throne - a very elaborate affair with lots of protrusions, statues and knobbly bits - not at all comfortable looking! As you leave the sanctuary to the left of the High Altar you may notice a portrait painting of a very striking and beautiful woman - Queen Saint Jadwiga (d 1399).

Zygmunt Bell Tower

Your self-conducted tour will now lead you through the Sacristy and up the Zygmunt Bell Tower. This is a real adventure! You will climb up a steep, creaky, wooden staircase, weaving your way round and through the massive criss-cross timber beams that support the tower - shined to a deep, smooth patina by the thousands of hands that have gripped as they have passed through. There is little concession to the rigours of EU Health and Safety here, which contributes hugely to the adventure and the charm! And on upwards, meeting, in 'close encounter' as you go, the five massive bells hanging one above the other in the tower, the biggest being the Zygmunt, cast in 1520 and weighing-in at 11 tons. Apparently it is only rung on major Church and National feast days. There are commanding views through the window at the top - to the right a mass of spires and domes of Old Kraków, and over to the left, the more prosaic suburbia and industrial landscape, with distant hills.

Altar of Jesus Crucified

Coming down from the Zygmunt Tower you resume your tour back down the left-hand ambulatory, where you will pass four side chapels dedicated to various cardinals and bishops to your left, the sacristy door, and then, at the end, on your left, at the junction with the transept behind the High Altar, the Altar of Jesus Crucified. This is a very striking depiction of the Crucifixion, with the sizeable Gothic Corpus and Cross carved in blackened wood (late 14th century) and set against a beaten and finely wrought silver sheet with a surround of black marble and gold embellishments, the whole being dramatically veiled by a thin gauze of black tulle. The sombre black and gold contrast vividly with the vibrant red altar cloth, red roses and red carpet - all portraying a powerful and dramatic scene. It was at this altar that Queen St Jadwiga prayed, frequently experiencing mystical visions.

That this altar continues to offer solace and inspiration is testified by the faithful who fervently kneel and pray here, and the votive offerings on display. The brightly lit reliquary under the altar contain the relics of Queen St Jadwiga.

Meditation before a Crucifix

The Saviour hangs before you with a pierced heart. He has spilled his heart's blood to win your heart. If you want to follow him in holy purity, your heart must be free of every earthly desire. Jesus, the Crucified, is to be the only object of your longings, your wishes, your thoughts...

It is the loving heart of your Saviour that invites you to follow. It demands your obedience because the human will is blind and weak. It cannot find the way until it surrenders itself entirely to the divine will...

The arms of the Crucified are spread out to draw you to his heart. He wants your life in order to give you his.

The world is in flames. The conflagration can also reach our house. But high above all flames towers the cross. They cannot consume it. It is the path from earth to heaven. It will lift one who embraces it in faith, love and hope into the bosom of the Trinity.

(St Teresa Benedicta of the Cross)

Side chapels and monuments

The chapel immediately next to this altar also caught my eye - dedicated to St Catherine - with its silver and black altar, finely vaulted and with a richly frescoed ceiling. Have a peep also at the chapel on the left as you pass behind the high altar - that of the Birth of the Virgin Mary - once the royal oratory, having been connected by a roofed gallery to the royal palace. It contains what is described as one of the finest examples of Mannerist (that art which is no longer perceived to exhibit the harmonious and rational approaches associated with the High Renaissance) sculptures of the reclining King Stefan Batory carved in red marble.

The next chapel, at the head of ambulatory that goes back down past the High Altar, is a chapel dedicated to St Thomas Becket - which got me thinking - and yes, although not obvious from commentary or trappings, it is dedicated to St Thomas Becket, Archbishop of Canterbury, martyred at his altar in 1170.

As you walk down this ambulatory you will notice on the right, the handsome red Hungarian marble and sandstone tomb of King Casimir the Great (d 1370), during whose reign the cathedral was consecrated. That Queen Jadwiga was a very beautiful woman is confirmed by her recumbent statue over her sarcophagus in white Carerra marble, found further down on the right at the end of the ambulatory. It is a picture of grace, beauty and serenity. Next to her is her funerary regalia, a Gothic sceptre and orb. Tradition has it that the modesty of this regalia is attributed to her having bequeathed all her jewellery to help fund the restoration of Kraków University.

Zygmunt Chapel

Just opposite the monument to Queen Jadwiga is the side chapel that the cathedral is probably most noted for - the Zygmunt Chapel (or in the guide book The Chapel of the Assumption of the BVM). It is hailed as one of the finest examples of Renaissance design and ornamentation in northern Europe. It was commissioned by King Zygmunt I, the Elder (1506-48) and designed and executed principally by the Italian architect Bartolomo Berrecci, being completed in 1533. From the outside it is the chapel with the golden cupola. What is most striking in the interior is the astonishingly effective contrast of the bright red marble of the statuary set against the intricately carved pale sandstone surrounds. The principal figures are that of Zygmunt I, and son Zygmunt August and wife Queen Anna. The other feature is the 16th century altarpiece made in Nuremberg. The open panels show scenes from the life of Our Lady wrought in silver gilt, and when closed, paintings by the artist George Pencz of the Passion, Death, Resurrection and Ascension. The attractive coffered dome is of patterned rosettes.

The next chapel, the Immaculate Conception (Waza) was quite difficult to view through the heavy screen, but my notebook comment was 'Ugh! - all black'! What made up for this though, was the chapel next to that (the Presentation), which was a cheerful but tasteful warm red, displaying lively art nouveau polychrome figures and designs on the vault and walls.

The next chapel that deserves a good study is the last one at the back of the cathedral, the Chapel of the Holy Cross and the Holy Spirit. It is the only mediaeval chapel where most of its original decoration has survived, with the walls and vault being decorated with Byzantine polychromy, having been completed in the late 15th century. Note, up in the centre of the vault, God the Father gazing benignly down on the world, surrounded by a dazzling array of apocalyptic beasts and angelic choirs. The chapel is redolent with monument and symbology. The striking art nouveau stained glass window shows the nailing of Christ to the Cross, and the discovery of the Holy Cross by St Helena. All-in-all a most glorious lesson in history and contrasting styles!

Crypts

Having crossed the main nave at the back of the cathedral, you will notice the lovely stained glass window of the Chapel of the Holy Trinity, also at the back and on the other side of the main entrance, before you go underground, through the Chapel of the Passion, to the crypts.

These are extensive, starting with St Leonard's Crypt, one of the surviving elements of the second, Romanesque cathedral. It is here that Poland resonates its rich, turbulent history with the mute testament of the tombs, sarcophagi and memorials of its many kings, queens, and heroic men and women.

It was the crypt of the first Marshal of the Independent Republic and Chief of State, Józef Piłsudski, the last crypt on leaving, that particularly caught my attention. It is brightly lit and fronted by heavy, wrought-iron gates with national and military themes; the simple, brightly be-flowered and be-ribboned, bronze coffin sits on a shallow, rough-carved stone plinth. On the bare stone-brick wall at the rear, a large bronze plaque, displaying crossed rifles, and above, a copy of the icon of Our Lady of the Gate of Dawn in Wilno, Lithuania. Many other plaques round the crypt, given by regiments, veteran and other public organisations, demonstrate the wide respect that this powerful and fierce military man, and ultimately dictator of Poland, arouses in the Polish public.

The Old Town of Kraków

The compact area of the Old Town of Kraków (Stare Miasto) allows you to cover quite a lot of ground in a reasonably short time and space. On your first visit, or if heading down from the Cathedral, one will inevitably head for the hub of the Old Town, the picturesque and sizeable mediaeval Main Square (Rynek Główny), with all its buzzing activity, reminiscent of Covent Garden.

Our Lady of the Assumption

Presiding at an angle over the Square, from one of the corners, is the graceful, mellow, red brick presence of the Basilica of Our Lady of the Assumption, with its two curiously asymmetrical towers. The current building is the second on site - being built from 1355 onwards to replace the earlier 13th century church destroyed by the Tartar invasions. It is acknowledged as one of the finest Gothic structures in the country, and holds some superb artistic treasures, among which the carvings of Wit Stwosz, a 15th century craftsman of German origin.

On first acquaintance you have the choice of entering either as a paying visitor through the Visitors' entrance to the side of the church, or through the obvious main entrance porch under the towers, to that part of the church which is reserved for the faithful who have come to pray in front of the Blessed Sacrament in the side chapel dedicated to Our Lady of Częstochowa at the rear of the church. I chose the latter, not actually knowing at the time that there was Adoration in progress, but mainly to get a feel for the place before committing to the commercial bit! Well worth doing - and it may be (as it was for me) a first exposure to the reverence of the Polish people as they came in, and knelt in silent, gazing prayer in front of the Blessed Sacrament. Also a sizeable portion of the church is reserved here, and one can wander quietly round in blissful flash-free silence, visually exploring.

Meditation

Hail, O Lady, holy Queen,
Mary, holy Mother of God:
you are the Virgin made Church
and the one chosen by the most Holy Father in heaven
whom he consecrated
with his most holy beloved Son
and with the Holy Spirit the Paraclete,
in whom there was and is
all the fullness of grace and every good.
Hail, his palace! Hail, his tabernacle!
Hail, his home! Hail, his robe!
Hail, his servant! Hail, his Mother!

*And hail all you holy virtues which
through the grace and light of the Holy Spirit
are poured into the hearts of the faithful
so that from their faithless state
you may make them faithful to God.*
(St Francis of Assisi)

Visitors' section

Inevitably though, it is the Visitors' bit that is of interest. The specific focus is generally on the huge altar piece carved by Wit Stwosz in the late 15th century. It is a lime wood polyptych (piece consisting of more than three panels joined by hinges or folds) measuring some 11m long and 12m high. It is considered one of the finest examples of late Gothic art in Europe, and surprisingly Stoss' first major commission, and some say, his finest. It consists of carved, gilded polychromatic scenes on folding panels showing the lives and events of Jesus and Mary - twenty four in all. The panels are fully opened up just before midday for viewing. The colour, detail and dynamics are exquisite and very realistic - a hallmark of Stoss, who based his figures on contemporary Krakowians. The central, largest panel shows the Dormition of Our Lady, and then rising up to her Glorious Assumption, and in the finial above, her Coronation. A detailed 'decode' of the panels is given in the guide leaflet.

There are nine side chapels and fourteen side altars to examine. Other items of interest include the large, ornate Renaissance *Ciborium* (Tabernacle) over a side altar, and the most expressive and real figure of the Crucified Christ, carved from a single block of limestone by Stoss, also displayed over one of the side altars. Although the church is quite dim inside, one can still appreciate the dazzling stained glass windows, some from the 14th century, and the detailed and colourful polychromatic designs adorning the walls. Also take a look up at the nave ceiling - a glorious vaulted and star spangled affair!

Apart from its beauty, the church is known nationally by the trumpet call made from the taller, multi-pinnacled tower, and broadcast live to the nation every day at midday. In fact the call is made every hour on the hour, and commemorates the trumpeter who valiantly warned the city of impending attack by the Tartars, and was cut off in mid call by an arrow in his neck; the call still stops at that moment. If you are standing in the right place outside when the call is made, cast an eye up at the tower - you might receive a cheery wave from the fireman trumpeter, high up in his turret!

The Church of St Barbara

Immediately next door to St Mary's is the church of St Barbara, built from the bricks left over from St Mary's. It has a lovely vaulted, unsupported ceiling, richly and brightly frescoed, predominantly in pink, contrasts with the gold and green altar surrounds. Mirrored windows high-up give an illusion of space. It is noted for its 15th century Pieta in stone, and 15th century crucifix on the high altar.

The Church of St Adalbert

Sitting at a jaunty angle in the square is the diminutive church of St Adalbert. The oldest building in the square, it rests on the site of the first church in Kraków. It has all the features of any larger sized church, including a minute dome and organ gallery. To me, this tiny church, dwarfed by its vast hedonistic surroundings, is a microcosm of the Church - perfect in content, perfect in what it offers, perfect in what it dispenses.

Contrasting Churches

A short walk from the square are two very contrasting, but nonetheless marvellous churches in their own right (and rite!), which ironically, sit on opposite sides of the same street: the Dominican church of the Holy Trinity and the Franciscan church of St Francis of Assisi.

The Dominican church of the Holy Trinity

The austere and beautifully ethereal Dominican church of the Holy Trinity, boasts an intricately and elaborately carved and richly decorated high altar, at the centre of which is a most dignified, serene but powerful depiction of the Holy Trinity. Side chapels of note are the exuberant Chapel of Our Lady of the Rosary, with crowned icon of a rosy-cheeked Madonna and Child; the Renaissance chapel to St Jacek (Hyacinth), and the rather dark-marbled, sombre chapel to St Dominic, contrasted by the luminous, embossed gold icon of the Saint above the altar.

The Franciscan church of St Francis of Assisi.

The Franciscan church of St Francis of Assisi is a celebration of the most dazzling and ebullient polychromatic display of colour and design: flowers, leaves, plants, zigzags, abstract motifs, eagles, all in tumbling profusion and bright contrasting colours over every square inch, but all somehow well ordered, geometric, thematic and coherent. It is a marvel of pattern and colour, vibrant and exciting. The whole is complemented by the dazzling art nouveau windows, of which the most striking is the rear window, entitled 'Let It Be'. It is all the work of the artist Stanislaw Wyspiański in the early 1900s, who at only twenty eight executed this daring, and probably at the time, rather risky, vast work of art, encompassing walls, windows and ceilings of this large building. Two major side chapels: the Chapel of the Lord's Passion, and, continuing the vibrant patterned motifs of the main church - the chapel of Our Lady of

Sorrows in which Exposition of the Blessed Sacrament takes place. There are bright airy cloisters to wander in.

The Church of St Andrew's

A few minutes' stroll away from these two churches, back down the central street Grodzka towards the Castle and Cathedral, will bring you to the imposing façade of the Church of Ss Peter and Paul. This magnificent early Baroque church was modelled on the Jesuit church *Il Gesu*, in Rome, but it is not as ornate. However, I particularly want to direct your attention to the rather unassuming, modest looking little 11th century church sitting quietly next door, St Andrew's.

This is my little gem in this part of my travels. From the outside it looks more like a sturdy fortress, with its blunt, patched walls, and twin, onion domed towers, pierced with defensive embrasures. And indeed it was a fortress, as it was reputedly the only church that withstood the Tartar invasion of 1241.

Inside it is tiny, but be prepared to be overwhelmed by Baroque in its fullest glory! Its crammed, glittering interior, is absolutely alive with pictures, statues, crowns, sunburst, cherubs - every single inch of everything gilded, patterned or painted - all coming tumbling at you from every direction! Fresh flowers also abound, no doubt placed by the Poor Clares, whose convent is next door, and who so lovingly tend this small church. I have got to say, despite Adoration being in progress, I just sat there open mouthed in part wonder, part glee, that so much could be packed into such a small space - and yet nothing seems superfluous.

It is centred by the dramatic silver and ebony Tabernacle at the altar which contrasts with the pastel frescoes in the apse, half-dome and barrelled ceiling. Have a close look at the extraordinary pulpit in the shape of a boat in full sail, complete with silver sails and gold rigging, and an angel seemingly doing a somersault of joy through the mainsail! See also the exquisite gilt framed organ loft.

Inevitably there will be places that I have had to omit through time and space restraints - apologies for that - no doubt you will find your own, and take as much joy as I have, over those described above.

Sanctuary of the Divine Mercy

"Many of my memories are connected with this place. I used to come here especially during the German occupation, when I was working in the nearby Solvay plant. I still remember that road leading from Borek Falecki to Debniki; I followed it every day in my wooden shoes... How could one imagine that this man in clogs will one day consecrate the Basilica of Divine Mercy in Kraków-Łagiewniki." These words of Pope John Paul II in August 2002 at the Dedication Mass for the new Divine Mercy Basilica in the Łagiewniki suburb of Kraków brought together many extraordinary strands woven by Divine Providence in conveying a powerful vehicle of God's Mercy to the world.

Foundation

The story starts, indirectly, with the foundation in 1862 of the Congregation of the Sisters of Our Lady of Mercy in Warsaw. The Congregation's apostolic mission was to run their Homes of Mercy: to house, educate and assist young women with troubled backgrounds. 1891 saw the foundation of their House at the current site in Kraków-Łagiewniki, and here today, as in their other houses, they continue with this same mission. It was this Congregation that Helen Kowalska entered in 1925, taking the religious name of Mary Faustina. And it was to Sister Faustina that Our Lord appeared in the image of the Divine Mercy, starting in 1931 and over the next seven years, revealing to her all those elements of the devotion to the Divine Mercy that are now practised so widely in the Universal Church. Faustina suffered ill health, including tuberculosis, and died in the Łagiewniki convent, aged 33 in 1938. She was canonised by Pope John Paul II in April 2000. (The Devotion to the Divine Mercy and Sister Faustina's life are described in detail in the CTS booklet *The Divine Mercy and St Faustina.*)

These revelations and Devotions were not without controversy in the early years, and tended to be confined to the Sisters' Congregations, and then spreading gradually to the Polish Armed Forces through their chaplains, and sporadically to other parts of the world by Polish emigrés. It was not until 1978, after extensive theological scrutiny of the far-reaching and deeply spiritual writings of this largely uneducated nun, that the ban imposed by the Holy See was lifted. The devotion developed a strong world-wide momentum, aided by the Apostolic Movement of the Divine Mercy, whose headquarters is at Łagiewniki. As the momentum grew, it became obvious that the modest Convent Chapel would be unable to cope with the ever increasing number of pilgrims. On the day of Our Lady's Nativity, 8th September, in 1999, construction started on the new Basilica. It was consecrated by Pope John Paul II on 17th August 2002.

The Basilica

On seeing the Basilica for the first time, one's first impression - and actually one that abides - is that of a majestic, modern ocean liner in full passage - and maybe that was the architectural intent, to portray one of the flagships of today's Church, fully underway. It is built in gleaming white, smooth stone and marble, elliptical in shape, canted from rear to front - further giving the impression of movement, and with a prominent 'bridge' superstructure (which floods the sanctuary beneath with light) at the rear. At the front, is a towering mast with a glass 'crow's nest', topped with a golden cross. At the foot of the mast, a fitting figurehead - a bronze statue of Pope John Paul II, looking boldly ahead at the course this ship will steer, robes billowing, arms widely outstretched: one in greeting, the other releasing a dove of peace.

Inside, an immense feeling of light and space. The whole church is of one nave - uncluttered by any pillars - a soaring roof, light pouring in from the plentiful plain vertical, full length windows. The simple semi-circular sanctuary is raised by a few steps on a white, shining marble plinth. The centre piece against the curve of the

Sanctuary, Shrine of the Divine Mercy (Łagiewniki, Kraków)

apse is the well known picture by Hyla, of Jesus of the Divine Mercy - right arm raised in blessing, left hand exposing the red ray of blood and the pale ray of water from His Heart. His eyes intent: serious, beckoning, beseeching, willing us to look into them, and then into His Heart. Below this picture - a prominent Tabernacle, in the shape and shades of a golden, global earth. Surrounding the Tabernacle and picture, a sizeable bronze sculpture of many, bare, swaying, windswept branches - our turbulent and often stark lives.

Standing right at the back, one can take in this magnificent temple, with its huge, radiating, crown-like pale, wooden ceiling beams, to the glowing, light-strewn apse, to the contrasting white and dark marble floor, with the dark strips leading one to the altar. There is an upper gallery and choir for a thousand people; the whole church can hold a congregation of five thousand.

Meditation

Sister Faustina writes in her Diary: *"In the evening, when I was in my cell, I saw the Lord Jesus clothed in a white garment. One hand [was] raised in the gesture of blessing, the other was touching the garment at the breast. From beneath the garment, slightly drawn aside at the breast, there were emanating two large rays, one red, the other pale. In silence I kept my gaze fixed on the Lord; my soul was struck with awe, but also with great joy. After a while, Jesus said to me, "Paint an image according to the pattern you see, with the signature: Jesus I trust in You. I desire that this image be venerated, first in your chapel, and [then] throughout the world. I promise that the soul that will venerate this image will not perish. I also promise victory over [its] enemies already here on earth, especially at the hour of death. I myself will defend it as my own Glory".*

Chaplet to the Divine Mercy

Using the Rosary, on the three single beads, begin with an *Our Father*, a *Hail Mary* and *The Apostles' Creed*.
At the beginning of each decade, on the single bead, pray:
Eternal Father, I offer You the Body and Blood, Soul and Divinity of Your dearly beloved Son, Our Lord Jesus Christ, in atonement for our sins and those of the whole world.
On each of the ten decade beads, pray:
For the sake of His sorrowful Passion, have mercy on us and on the whole world.
Conclude by praying three times:
Holy God, Holy Mighty One, Holy Immortal One,
Have mercy on us and on the whole world.

Below the main church there is another sizeable indoor gathering area, with a central chapel (dedicated to St Faustina), and four other modern, well appointed side chapels, for smaller, visiting groups.

Adoration Chapel

Separate from, but immediately next to the Basilica, is a small Adoration Chapel, in which continuous Adoration takes place. It is the sweetest of places in which to adore the Lord. Circular, with a striking open, pale bronze sculpture holding the Blessed Sacrament, either as gentle enfolding hands, or the petals of a graceful, opening flower. The Host is encased in the most glorious and intricate gold and silver-gilt monstrance. Narrow, vertical, colourful and tasteful nouveau-art windows surround the chapel, and there are always beautiful flowers at the foot of the Lord. Any time, any day, any night, the chapel is open for Adoration.

Adoration Meditation

*"My heart is drawn here where my God is hidden,
Where He dwells with us day and night,
Clothed in the White Host;
He governs the whole world, He communes with souls.*

*My heart is drawn here where my God is hiding,
Where His love is immolated.
But my heart senses that the living water is here;
It is my living God, though a veil hides Him."*

(St Faustina)

The other modern buildings surrounding the Basilica are meeting halls, a shopping arcade, and the large Pastoral Centre, with very pleasant and reasonable pilgrim accommodation and restaurant facilities. A ride up the lift (or you can climb the 315 stairs) to the 'crow's nest' at the top of the 'mast' is a must, giving magnificent and contrasting views of industrialisation round Kraków and the contrasting soft greenery of country the side and distant Tatra hills.

Wandering around the extensive grounds you will come across the Sisters' cemetery, the Stations of the Cross, and the original field altar, set well away from the Basilica next to the convent, but still used for smaller outdoor gatherings.

Convent Chapel

One's attention can now turn to the original convent chapel, dedicated to St Joseph, and in which St Faustina's remains are interred. Consecrated in 1891, this simple attractive, red-bricked chapel was to become the centre of major attention. Despite this, it is well organised and reverently run. You are greeted by a high, gabled frontage with entrance and narthex. A simple square tower with pointed copper clad roof is visible. This simple, humble exterior belies the most gorgeous chapel inside. It is well worth an in-depth examination!

On entering, your eyes may well be drawn straight down the aisle to the apse and carved wooden altar, above which a graceful, all-white statue of Our Lady, with gold-edged robes, gazing down on the tabernacle, below. Look now to the side altar on the left hand side. There you will see, with a sense of thrill, an original of the famous Hyła picture of the Divine Mercy. This was the second picture he painted, as a votive offering for saving his family during the war, specifically designed to fit the niche above this altar. Below the picture is the small, brightly lit sarcophagus of Saint Faustina's mortal remains, invariably framed by beautiful arrangements of flowers. Her head-and-shoulders portrait sits to the left of the altar. In front of this altar, at the communion rail, a relic is displayed in a small marble, glass fronted stand, for the faithful to kneel, pray and kiss.

Your next level of consciousness may now focus on the array of wood-framed, red baize cases that line the walls of the chapel in profusion and in all shapes and sizes. In a very continental fashion, these are the thousands of votive offerings presented by individuals to the chapel in grateful thanks for Saint Faustina's intercessions of prayer and prayer requests. They are most beautifully and skilfully displayed and arranged. The majority of the offerings are small silver hearts aflame, but there are also hundreds of other precious items: pearl and amber necklaces, rings, medallions, crosses, platelets, shields - all in precious materials - all cleverly arranged in striking patterns and designs. These alone are worth admiring and appreciating.

Now looking wider and higher, you will notice the vibrant, art nouveau style of bright, polychrome, geometric multi-coloured patterns decorating the walls and vault, very similar to that of the Franciscan church in Kraków. I found this style of decoration very beautiful and lively, but without being jarring, and adding a further sense of joy and a unique brightness to the building.

Meditation

Although uncomfortable, it may be worth meditating, here in St Faustina's 'home', the vision of hell that she saw:

'Today, I was led by an angel to the chasms of hell. It is a place of great torture; how awesomely large and extensive it is! The kinds of tortures I saw: the first torture that constitutes hell is the loss of God; the second is perpetual remorse of conscience; the third is that one's condition will never change; the fourth is the fire that will penetrate the soul without destroying it - a terrible suffering, since it is a purely spiritual fire, lit by God's anger; the fifth torture is a continual darkness and a terrible suffocating smell, and, despite the darkness, the devils and the souls of the damned, see each other and all evil, both of others and their own; the sixth torture is the constant company of Satan; the seventh torture is horrible despair, hatred of God, vile words, curses and blasphemies. These are the tortures suffered by all the damned together, but that is not the end of the sufferings. There are special tortures destined for particular souls.

These are the torments of the senses. Each soul undergoes terrible and indescribable sufferings, related to the manner in which it has sinned. There are caverns and pits of torture where one form of agony differs from another. I would have died at the very sight of these tortures if the omnipotence of God had not supported me. Let the sinner know that he will be tortured throughout all eternity in those senses which he made use of to sin. I am writing this at the command of God, so that no soul may find an excuse by saying there is no hell, or that nobody has ever been there, and so no one can say what it is like.' (St Faustina)

Prayer

"You urge me to be merciful in three ways. First in merciful action, whatever it might be. Secondly, in merciful words; if I cannot help through actions, I will help with my words. The third thing is prayer. If I cannot show mercy either through actions, or through words, I will always be able to do it through my prayer, for prayer reaches where I cannot reach myself. O my Jesus, transfigure me into Yourself, for You can do everything."
(St Faustina)

Nowa Huta and the Salt Mines

The immediate environs of Kraków provide some fruitful pilgrim venues of interesting and contrasting character - two new churches built out of adversity during the communist regime; other more mature churches, but also contrasting and intriguing; a large underground salt mine, complete with unique chapel - probably the only one like it in the world; and a peaceful, 11th century fortified Benedictine river-side monastery.

Nowa Huta

One of the suburbs of Kraków is Nowa Huta - 'New Town' - a vast residential and industrial complex built from scratch by the Communist regime in the late 1940s. It was a social engineering exercise designed to counterbalance the predominant (and intellectually resistant) middle class intelligentsia of Kraków with a large injection of 'the working class', who no doubt would be loyal to the Socialist ideal. A huge steelworks was built as the focus of work, and round it endless streets of uniform grey-slabbed residential blocks of flats radiating out from Plac Centralny, a vast hexagonal area, in what has been described as a 'gargantuan Stalinist re-working of

Renaissance ideals'. In fact what this influx brought was a politically and actively resistant segment of the population, fuelled by their faith to the Church and manifested by Solidarity (Solidarność) - forming, with the original Krakowians, a perfect 'double whammy' of resistance to the Communist regime.

As a witness to the desires of the faithful during this period there rose two amazing new churches - both built by the drive and vision of their respective parish priest, with the strong support of the then Archbishop of Kraków, Karol Wojtyla; both were built by the efforts - financial and physical - of the parishioners. The better known of these churches is the extraordinary Arka Pana, the Ark of the Lord, formally the Church of Our Lady Queen of Poland, and, the not quite so well known St Maximillian Kolbe Church, in the nearby suburb of Mistrzejowice.

Arka Pana

When you catch sight of the Arka Pana you know you are going to experience something very different. For, seemingly docked on top of the huge smooth, sweeping curves of the church walls is the hull of an enormous boat. Reaching up above this unusual roofline is a slender 70 metre-high mast, with cross and golden crown, and which architecturally anchors the construction of the whole church together: reality portraying powerful symbolism.

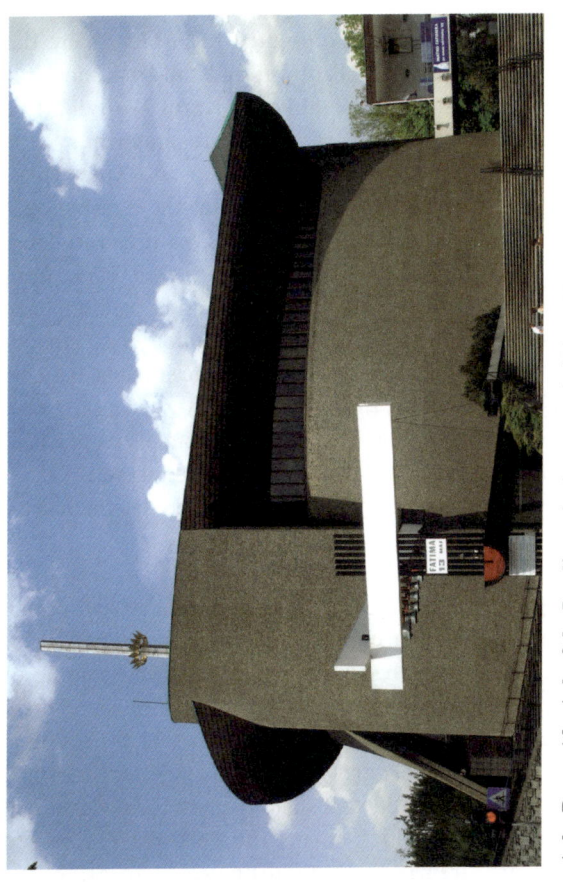

Arka Pana - 'the Ark of the Lord' - at the 'new town' of Nowa Huta

This extraordinary building was started in 1967, the first stone having been presented to Fr Gorzelany, the parish priest, by Pope Paul VI, and the first shovelful having been dug by Archbishop Karol Wojtyla. The Government refused to hire out machinery for construction - bare hands raised the steelwork, wheelbarrows humped the concrete; the nearby steel works was forbidden to sell the steel, so it had to come from much further afield; voluntary workers came from all over the world to help with construction, as did money and gifts, small and large. The two million or so smooth river pebbles cladding the exterior were brought back by parishioners from the mountain rivers - again in a symbolic 'body of the church' gesture, but also a practical defence against the nearby heavily polluting steel works. In May 1977 Cardinal Wojtyla consecrated the sanctuary.

Inside

I suspect, on entry, your eye will immediately fall on the large, dramatic, arched, bronze sculpture of Christ Crucified seemingly being launched into the middle of the congregation from the left hand side of the church. Having registered that, you will notice that the inside is vast, plain, with pale grey décor, in a single-naved format, with the front, curved wall slanting up to the underside of the ark's hull, which forms the ceiling. The raised sanctuary area is free-standing, so as to allow the congregation to surround it. There is a large mezzanine gallery on the left to allow for extra seating capacity.

The altar is a single, massive slab of white Carrera marble; the Tabernacle, to the left, is a rough hewn bronze globe supported by a simple cross. Embedded in its doors, is a rutile crystal brought from the moon by the crew of Apollo 11 and presented to Pope Paul VI, who gave it to Fr Gorzelany. A huge organ of 4,500 pipes is at the back; on the left wall of the nave is a very striking Stations of the Cross painted in the early 1980s by the artist Mariusz Lipinski. It depicts a flowing sequence of sometimes two Stations on the same picture, all progressing through a bleak and bare Polish countryside, with most of the figures going about their daily lives indifferent to the dramatic goings on around them.

Underneath the main church are two chapels. The first, smaller chapel, dedicated to Our Lady of Fatima, is open for daily Adoration. The second, larger chapel, was closed when I visited, but on seeking out the Sister in the Sacristy, she found me a kind man who opened up and conducted me round this sombre chapel of Reconciliation. It is well worth a good examination. It is low-ceilinged, and by design, of low light level. It is remarkable for the many expressive variations of Pieta on display. Amongst the other statues are: one of Our Lady, made of artillery shell casings and bomb fragments found by Polish soldiers at Monte Cassino, and presented by

Poles living in Australia; a dramatic bronze of St Maximillian Kolbe - to whom the chapel is dedicated - in his Auschwitz uniform, and an unusual statue of Jesus with Mary Magdalene. On the entrance to the chapel are written the words: "Before entering this chapel you must reconcile with God, with your neighbour and with yourself". The many confessionals lining one of the chapel walls reinforces this.

Church dedicated to St Maximillian Kolbe

Not far from the Arka Pana in Mistrzejowice, is the church dedicated to St Maximillian Kolbe. The vision of the parish priest at the time, Father Józef Kurzega, it was built in the early 1980s against the odds of communist obstruction, and consecrated by Pope John Paul II in 1983. A complete contrast to the Arka Pana - a church of 'angles and arrowheads', with its lofty ceiling of arrowhead shaped buttresses, arrowhead floor plan and angular sanctuary area with dramatic bronze Crucifix. At the back are two side chapels: on the left, to the Risen Christ, depicted by an eloquent bronze statue; and to the right a Lady Chapel with a tranquil statue of Our Lady. Underneath is a quiet, subdued, low-ceilinged crypt chapel.

Contrasting churches

In complete contrast to these two modern churches, and close to the Nowa Huta area, are the 13th century

Cistercian Abbey at Mogiła (the Sanctuary of the Holy Cross), and just opposite, the diminutive, all-wood, 15th century church of St Bartholomew.

Cistercian Abbey at Mogiła

This tranquil Abbey and Monastery, within its suburban surrounds, is set in extensive and peaceful gardens around which you can wander, admiring the ingenious garden architecture displaying just about every shape, size and colour of pine and fir trees - all beautifully done. The handsome three-naved Abbey church is well known for its mediaeval wooden Crucifix - the Miraculous Christ - which survived a fire in 1447. It is displayed in a glittering green and gold side chapel. The arched, nave ceilings of the main church are beautifully decorated with polychrome. Above the high altar is a 16th century triptych featuring a statue of the Madonna and Child, with scenes from the Holy Family and the Passion.

The Church of St Bartholomew

The small church opposite, St Bartholomew's, is a real treat! Its total construction is of wood - from the ornate onion-domed gate porch, to the main building, from roof tiles downwards. Its rather drab exterior is belied inside with an explosion of exuberance and bright colour from floor to ceiling, even the pews are brightly painted! A charming, eccentric and unique building that barely gets a mention in the mainstream guide books, but well worth a visit, providing real contrast to any other church that you will see on your Polish pilgrimage.

Benedictine Monastery at Tyniec

Just south west of the outskirts of Kraków is the Benedictine Monastery at Tyniec. The Monastery goes back to 1044, and the present buildings have emerged from four episodes of severe damage since that time. The monastery complex is a compact and sturdy fortress-like affair, set on a defensive bluff dominating the River Wisła below. The Abbey church is in the Gothic style, with a mainly Baroque interior. It has an impressive black marble high altar, contrasted by gold statues, and with a picture of Saints Peter and Paul as the centrepiece. There are six side chapels off the side naves, the two central ones being dedicated to St Benedict, and St Scholastica, his sister. There is a delightful small terrace restaurant with lovely views of the river below. A tranquil place.

The Salt Mines

A visit to the salt mines just to the south of Kraków is a must. Salt has been mined from the huge underground deposit at Wieliczka from the 11th century. Owing to the value of this commodity the mines were owned and controlled by the Crown. Commercial mining has now

St Kinga's underground chapel deep in the Salt Mines, Wieliczka

ceased; it is a UNESCO World Heritage site, and today its sole income is from tourism. It is certainly an unusual venue - a tour of some two hours along a two kilometre underground route going to a depth of 135 metres. One has to go with a guide, and English speaking tours are scheduled throughout the day in the high season. Initial descent is down many wide wooden steps, and consists of an ever descending visit to the many carved-out chambers en route, all depicting aspects and activities of salt mining. Some of the chambers are vast and spectacular, reaching high up into the gloom, some with brine lakes of deep green, luminescent water, all lit to dramatic effect. Our English speaking guide had all the expected wisecracks to entertain us with, but also the expected in-depth knowledge of his subject to inform us - the two hours flew by. There is also the reassurance of toilet stops en route!

St Kinga's Chapel

To me the most spectacular and awe inspiring of these chambers is the St Kinga's Chapel at the 135 metre level. It is a large chamber, over 50 metres long, 18 metres wide and up to 12 metres high. It is a fully furnished and detailed chapel - all completely carved out of salt - the ceiling, the shining faux-tile floor, the statues, the balustrades, the altar, the pulpit, the Papal throne, the Crucifix. At this stage we were beginning to learn that salt, in a mine like this, is as hard and as durable as rock. This beautiful 'working' chapel is the miners' thanks to God for their lives and livelihood. The sculptures - intricate, detailed and striking - are all the work of skilled miners throughout the years. Note the dramatic way that St Kinga, a 13th century Royal Queen, canonised by Pope John Paul II in 1999, is displayed above the high altar; and also the luminescent statue of Our Lady of Lourdes, demonstrating that not only is salt durable, but translucent as well.

There is also an underground cafeteria and museum at which you can extend your underground stay after the tour. For those who are of a claustrophobic disposition or slightly nervous of lifts, you must brace and prepare yourselves for a few moments of bravery for the return trip. This is made in a double-decker, rather low-tech, miners' lift, into which you are shoehorned, and up which you are transported at high speed, whistling exhilaratingly up the darkened lift shaft. It was a fitting end to a very good tour, and did wonders for a final group bonding! I did have a very careful look at the winding wheel, mechanism and cable when I had got to the top - it all looked reassuringly robust and sturdy!

Kalwaria Sanctuary and Wadowice

Papal Train

There are two other places outside Kraków well worth visiting and that are conveniently linked by a rather special train. Both places can be taken in on a day's return outing from Kraków, either leaving from Kraków Station, or, jumping on as it calls by at Łagiewniki station, in the Kraków suburbs, where the Shrine of the Divine Mercy is located. The train is the 'Papal Train' (Pociąg Papieski), a sleek, modern, custom designed, silver and gold train that runs from Kraków to Wadowice, Pope John Paul II's birthplace, via Kalwaria Zebrzydowska, where there is a sizeable Franciscan monastery and an extensive 'cross country' Stations of the Cross (Kalwaria). The train, with its smart papal colours, comfortable seats and large video screens showing episodes of John Paul II's journeys, was the idea and initiative of Polish railway workers in 2005, who wanted to commemorate, in their own way, the pontificate of their Polish Pope. In itself, it is rather a special outing, with a happy pilgrim atmosphere, crewed by a team who are obviously proud of their train, and affording some relaxing views of the Polish countryside as one rumbles along, listening to the excited chatter of Polish, and international pilgrims.

Kalwaria

You can break your journey at Kalwaria, and make the half hour walk up the hill to the monastery, just the other side of the town. The Kalwaria sanctuary dates back to 1600. It is a significant place of pilgrimage for Polish people, and increasingly, international pilgrims; Pope John Paul II visited as a boy, priest, archbishop and Pope, and Pope Benedict XVI came here on his Polish tour. It is particularly well known for its fervent and whole scale re-enactment of the Passion during Holy Week, and devotions to Our Lady during the Assumption. Because of its outstanding and unusual combination of architecture, landscape and pilgrim venue it is a listed UNESCO World Heritage site.

The whole project of the church and monastery, and accompanying Calvary, was initiated by a local nobleman, Mikołaj Zebrzydowski in 1600. Mikołaj was convinced that the topography of his lands was similar to Jerusalem, and therefore suitable to lay down a Calvary route that followed Our Lord's Passion. This was very much in the mediaeval tradition, where for whatever reason one could not make it to Jerusalem, the next best thing was to follow the Passion in a close geographical and architectural reconstruction.

Our Lady of the Angels

The present-day Basilica, dedicated to Our Lady of the Angels, is in the late Baroque style, and has seen continuous development, additions and extensions over the centuries. It is in the care, and has been since 1601, of the Franciscans (OFM), known locally as the Bernadines. As you approach, you notice on your right, a rather homely, brightly be-flowered terrace of rustic houses, then up some wide cobbled steps into a spacious, enclosed square in front of the Basilica, also noting the numerous confessionals ranged round the covered side-arcades. The plain, rendered, light coloured façade effectively sets off the twin towers with their darker, copper-encased onion domes.

Inside the single-naved Basilica, and once your eyes have adjusted to the light, you realise what a blaze of colour it all is. The subtly vaulted ceiling is awash with a light blue 'sky' and frescoes of local scenes, the Holy Trinity and Our Lady's life. The high altar, in '*baldacchino*' style', framed by its twisting gold pillars, is a fantastic blaze of silver and gold: a large silver embossment of the Madonna and Child against a contrasting red background above the tabernacle, and a huge exploding sunburst of golden rays, encircling Christ the King, above it all. Before you explore the side chapels and altars, turn, and view the elaborately decorated organ loft at the back, with its modern, stained glass window.

The side chapel of most interest is rather inconspicuously tucked away off the sanctuary to the left - I had to ask to find it. In here the image of Our Lady of Kalwaria is venerated, and has been since 1641, starting a great Marian devotion, as well as the special commemorations of Christ's Passion. With the miracles attributed by the faithful to Our Lady's intercession through this icon - as witnessed by the many votive offerings on display in the chapel - it remains the centre of fervent devotion to Our Lady. It is a small oval, be-pillared chapel, the focus of which is the Madonna and Child above the chapel's small altar. As with Częstochowa, Pope John Paul II presented a gold Papal Rose to the Basilica, "...as a sign of gratitude for what she was, and has never stopped being, in my life".

Calvary Way

Outside, there are actually two routes along the Calvary Way - one commemorating Our Lord's Passion with the Stations of the Cross (red signs 'Dróżki Pana Jezusa'), and the other dedicated to Our Lady with events linked to her (blue signs 'Drózkí Matki Bożej') . The paths of these two intermingle all the way round, and although quite ambitious, it is possible to visit all 41 chapels, buildings and structures depicting both Ways. These chapels come in various shapes and sizes, some very elaborate (described somewhat irreverently as 'bonsai cathedrals'), others very simple; some plain, some in quite intriguing shapes and designs - but all in miniature perfection. They are all placed in a tranquil rural setting of some six square kilometres, sometimes passing by peaceful rustic homes. Although it can be busy around the Basilica and nearby Stations, the outer reaches are peaceful. If you have time, and wish to fully savour this quite unique setting, I would recommend a good day's worth here.

The whole is a sizeable complex, spaciously set in lovely grounds, and there are other nooks and crannies in and round the Basilica and monastery that will take a good exploring! There is a shop and very reasonable restaurant.

Wadowice

Just down the line, a short distance away, is the small, charming town of Wadowice, where Pope John Paul II was born in 1920. The town centre is a short, ten minute walk from the station. I was immediately struck by the clear signing to various places of interest in the town, indicative of a place that is going to greet and guide its many guests right at the outset. And thus it was - one can navigate around quite easily.

Basilica of the Presentation

The centre of attraction, sitting squarely at the head of the small town park, is the Basilica of the Blessed Virgin Mary's Sacrifice (or Presentation), the church where Pope

John Paul used to attend and pray as a boy. From the outside it is an unusual, seemingly unbalanced looking church, quite Eastern in looks, with the large copper, onion dome atop the square, pillared clock tower. This is the third church to sit on this site, built in late Baroque style, being consecrated in 1808. It is handsome rather than beautiful: stone work of gleaming white pillars and balustrades, with pale grey panels.

Inside it glows. The whole is tastefully decorated in a subtle ochre and lemon polychrome marbled effect. On the ceiling of the main nave, in vivid colours, are lively and powerful depictions of Pope John Paul's Encyclicals. The apse is multi-vaulted and square pillared, centred by a large silver embossment of the Madonna and Child, set against a lustrous gold background.

Side Chapels

The side chapel to the left rear of the church is of particular interest - that of the Mother of God of Perpetual Help - for it is here that Karol Wojtyła prayed as a boy. Again, I can only describe it as golden and glowing. The focus in this chapel is the icon of the Madonna and Child, crowned by Pope John Paul in 1999, with the gold crowns made from gold jewellery given by parishioners. By the side of the picture hangs the Pope's rosary, and, rather intriguingly, at top right is displayed a Swiss alarm clock, given to the Pope by the citizens of Lourdes in

2004. As with so many churches and chapels in Poland, it was lovely to be able to spend some time in Adoration at this side chapel.

The place that particularly touched me was the ornate baptismal font in the Chapel of the Holy Family, where the Pope was baptised. There is a lovely photograph associated with this font of the Pope kneeling deeply and humbly at its foot, and at which he prayed, "...with filial devotion I kiss the doorstep of my family home, expressing my gratitude to God's Providence for the gift of life...for the warmth of my hometown, for the love of my family and friends. With deep worship I also kiss the threshold of the House of God. With child's trust I turn my eyes to the face of Our Lady of Perpetual Help in her image here in Wadowice".

Another side chapel - right rear - is dedicated to the Servant of God, John Paul II. It is still under development, but displayed a large portrait of John Paul II, looked over by realistic tailors' dummies in the uniform of the Swiss Papal Guard, and will display further papal artefacts in due course.

The church is well geared to visitors, with good English language guide booklets.

Museum

Next to the church, at Kościelna 7, on the top floor, is the two bedroomed flat where the Wojtyła family lived, and where Karol, the second son and youngest child, was born in a tiny room between the kitchen and the sitting room. The original apartment has been expanded into an eight room museum, and displays a large selection of memorabilia, both secular and religious.

It is beautifully and tastefully presented and laid out, with many items of fascination - large and small - portraying a multi-talented, active man. The item that struck me most was his brown scapular, on display in Room No 8 - a small, seemingly innocuous, simple little item, which when worn is hidden, but which actually displays huge trust and fidelity. You will be invited to don felt overslippers, in which you glide around the beautifully maintained parquet floor!

The Church of St Peter the Apostle

The large, modern church of St Peter the Apostle is just a short stroll from the town centre. It was built as a votive offering by the citizens of Wadowice in thanksgiving for their fellow citizen being elected to the Holy See, it being consecrated by Pope John Paul in 1991. It is a vast, lofty, single naved building, with a striking sanctuary, and an overall architectural theme boldly displaying contrasting circles and triangles, and dramatic hanging half pillars. The two side chapels are dedicated to Our Lady of Fatima and the Divine Mercy. Outside there is a well tended, spacious garden area with Stations of the Cross, and a grotto of Our Lady of Fatima. The rear of the church, in complete contrast to the flat front, is a dizzying cascade of half-coned, copper roofs, pierced by small protruding gables and inset windows.

Three places worth a visit

Whilst not on the international 'mainstream' pilgrim trail there are other places that would be worthy of a visit if time was on your side, or if for whatever reason you happened to be travelling in the vicinity:

Warsaw

Close to the Old Town (Stare Miasto), is the Gothic-style Cathedral of St John's, with next door, the Jesuit church dedicated to Our Lady of Charity. In the Żoliborz District, there is the church of St Stanisław Kostka ('Sanctuary of Conscience'), the parish church of Fr Jerzy Popiełuszko, who publicly preached against communism and was brutally murdered in 1984 by the state police. His cause for beatification is under way.

Licheń

East of Poznań and 15 kms north of Konin is the magnificent Basilica to Our Lady of Sorrows, Queen of Poland, seemingly rising out of the middle of nowhere. It is the seventh biggest church in Europe, seating 20,000 worshippers, the dream and fulfilment of 'Marians of the Immaculate' priest, Fr Makulski, who inspired the design and the construction and raised the funds. It houses a tiny miraculous portrait of Our Lady brought to Licheń by a soldier returning from the Napoleonic wars. It was consecrated in 2004, and after Częstochowa, is the second most popular pilgrim destination for Poles, with over a million pilgrims visiting each year.

Zakopane

In this picturesque hiking and ski resort in the foothills of the beautiful scenery of the Tatra mountains is the Sanctuary of Our Lady of Fatima. It was built by parishioners as a votive of thanksgiving for Pope John Paul's survival from the attempt on his life. It is a striking looking church with a huge conical roof and a slender, round, ribbed tower, and inside, fabulous stained glass windows. It offers lovely views of the surrounding countryside.

Our Lady of Częstochowa

The wide, Parisian-style, tree-lined boulevard that is Częstochowa's main street leads directly to the foot of the hill that overlooks this sprawling, modern town. On top of this hill, dominating the local skyline, sits the fortified Pauline monastery of Jasna Góra ('Bright Hill'), its elegant, tiered bell tower reaching delicately skyward. The Pauline monks established their monastery and a small church dedicated to Our Lady here in 1382.

The Black Madonna

Soon after, the precious icon of the Madonna and Child, captured from war with Ruthenia, was presented by Prince Władysław Opolczyk to the Paulines at Częstochowa for safe keeping. The provenance of the icon is shrouded by legend and tradition, in that it was painted by St Luke and came to Ruthenia via Jerusalem and Constantinople, already proving to be the focus of miraculous intervention. A more scientific approach has dated this icon to between the 6th and 9th centuries. Its iconic style is that of a typical 9th century Byzantine '*Hodegitria*' - 'She who points the Way', of which earlier prototypes and tradition takes its origin back to that of St Luke. It is known as the Black

Madonna purely through the original dark countenance of Mother and Child, no doubt further darkened by centuries of candle smoke and incense! As the monastery guide book points out, most other major Marian sites attracting the millions of visitors are usually associated with an apparition of Our Lady - but not Jasna Góra - it is the power, mystery and miraculous intervention associated with the image that draws the faithful.

With its strategic position in the local area, the monastery itself has been the subject of attacks, raids and sieges throughout the centuries, and with every subsequent episode, developing its fortress-like walls and ramparts. In one episode in 1430 a band of Hussites ransacked the monastery, severely damaging the icon. It was faithfully restored, and again legend has it that the three clearly visible scars on her right cheek (two vertical, one horizontal) inflicted in this raid, have always reappeared, despite restoration efforts.

In modern times 'sieges' have also been laid against Częstochowa, Poland, and the free world - namely fascism and communism These were also lifted, and many of the Polish faithful would say that the fascist scourge and the communist monolith were shattered by Our Lady's faithful intercession in response to the prayers of the faithful.

Since these times, Jasna Góra, with Our Lady of Częstochowa, has been the spiritual heartbeat of the Polish nation, and still remains the centre of massed Catholic devotion for Poles - wherever in the world they may be.

Monastery

Although seemingly compact, the monastery complex is actually quite spacious, with plenty of room to wander the wide ramparts. The surrounding grounds are also spacious, providing the area for the hundreds of thousands of pilgrims who converge below the outdoor altar on Our Lady's Feast days, particularly the Assumption, when the national pilgrimage takes place.

The principal entrance to the monastery is from the park areas below, where, as you approach, you will notice at the foot of the gates, a large bronze monument of Cardinal Stefan Wyszyński, head bowed, humbly kneeling before this sanctuary of Our Lady, who gave him, and the nation, such succour during the communist era. On approaching the entrance one is greeted by four successive gates leading up to the monastery, and between the third and fourth, the bridge over what was the moat. The other entry gate, John Paul II Gate, heads in from the main car parks and the sizeable Pilgrim Lodge and restaurant, and site shops, from the other side. On entering, rather than head straight for the Chapel of Our Lady, my own instinct was to savour the moment of arrival by wandering the perimeters and getting a feel for this holy place at a reflective pace.

Here, one senses the protection that this neat, elegant complex of contrasting red brick and copper roofed buildings provided during the sieges and wars. An exploration round the ramparts reveal a powerful, life-sized Stations of the Cross situated round the moat area, with many groups following them, praying down on them from the ramparts. Then the outdoor altar, looking down on the extensive park area and town below, and finally, the four prominent, defensive bastions, one at each corner, in which one of them - the Holy Trinity Bastion - a seven metre high, red bronze statue of Pope John Paul II, the pilgrim Pope, who came here six times during his reign to honour Our Lady, and give hope and inspiration to his suffering nation.

Chapel of Our Lady of Częstochowa

At last, the moment to go into the Chapel of Our Lady of Częstochowa. One enters through an enclosed courtyard, and then a large entrance vestibule with bright, stained glass windows. This chapel was built in the mid 17th century in the Renaissance style. It is not big, but it somehow seems to cope with the crowds, and does impart an air of comfortable intimacy. Of course, your eye heads straight through the large, ornate wrought iron grille into the sanctuary, and there, bordered by the starkly contrasting black and silver altar surrounds - is the icon.

It is challenging to think that from this one image flows such grace and power from God as to inspire individuals, and a nation, and is the wellspring of miraculous happenings, told and untold, as witnessed by the countless thousands of votive offerings festooning the walls of the church. She may not be the most beautiful Madonna - but icons are not about evoking shallow, surface emotions. As explained in his excellent CTS booklet *Icons*, Fr John Baggley makes clear, "...holy icons are often referred to as doors or windows: something through which we pass to another place, or through which we look into another world". Not being familiar (or sometimes even comfortable) with icons, our Western Church culture requires a bit of work to be done to appreciate that these holy images, "present us with persons and events seen in the light of the transfiguring and redeeming grace of God". And as we ourselves attempt to work at this, in this Chapel, one can see, from those faithful people kneeling before and gazing up at the Madonna and Child, that they are well through that door.

Just to the left of the icon is a golden sceptre and apple - the insignia of the Queen of Poland - the gold having been donated by a Polish women's group; on the right is the rare Papal Golden Rose, presented by Pope John Paul II, with his own votive offering, a golden heart with his personal motto *Totus tuus*.

The rest of the chapel is a treasure trove worth examining in detail. There are six side altars, two most striking being the altar of the Pieta, and the altar of the Holy Cross, featuring a 15th century crucifix. The vaulted ceiling is richly frescoed and embellished, and if you look back you will see a gorgeous organ gallery of cream and gold, with intricate fretting, delicate fresco inlays, cherubs aplenty and the serried, sized ranks of silver organ pipes.

There are frequent, set Mass times, but in between they seemed non-stop as well! Also be aware that the icon is covered (or 'veiled') for a short period in the middle of the day. It is worth going to the 'unveiling', which is done with great drama and ceremony, the highlight being a tremendous trumpet and booming drum fanfare as the richly embossed 17th century silver screen silently glides upwards, gradually revealing the icon. Note also that it is only the faces and hands of Jesus and Mary that are visible, the richly embellished and bejewelled surround is an 'overlay', donated by Pope Pius X in 1910. There are other fabulous overlays, ranging from the diamond robe to the ruby robe, even a military one, made up of a profusion of medals and crosses donated by soldiers. Every evening the icon is veiled finally for the day in a ceremony and prayer known as the Jasna Góra Appeal.

Act of Consecration

Pray accept my praise O blessed Mother,
O Immaculate Conception, Queen of Heaven and Earth refuge of sinners, and our most loving mother.
God has willed to entrust the entire order of mercy to you. Poor sinners, we cast ourselves at your feet, humbly imploring you to take us, with all that we are and have, wholly to yourself as your possession and property.
Make of us, of all our powers of soul and body, of our whole life, death and eternity, whatever most pleases you.
If it pleases you, use all that we are and have without reserve, wholly to accomplish what is said of you:
"the woman will crush the serpent's head", and
"you alone will destroy all heresies in the whole world".
May we become in your Immaculate and most merciful hands instruments of your love, ready to fully enkindle and bring to new life so many strayed and lukewarm souls. Thus will the reign of the Divine Heart of Jesus be extended without end.
Truly your presence alone restores the graces, bringing souls to conversion and holiness, since it is through your maternal hands that grace comes to us, flowing from the Divine Heart of Jesus. (St Maximillian Kolbe)

The Basilica

Whilst the centre of veneration is at the Chapel of Our Lady, one should not neglect the splendid Baroque Basilica of the Finding of the Holy Cross and Nativity of Our Lady, next door. It is an impressive example of Baroque art, built in the late 16th, early 17th centuries. The altar and apse depicting the Assumption are fantastically alive and full of vigorous activity. A beautiful gold Tabernacle is sheltered under the long drapes of a golden tent, topped with a Queen's crown, and being held open by many cherubs. Our Lady is borne aloft by angels, whilst the Holy Trinity and the rest of the Heavenly Host look down in joy at this Glorious Assumption.

There is plenty more to explore. A Knight's Hall and Refectory, Sacristy, Library and Arsenal. A clanging climb up the many steel steps of the bell tower is recommended. With limited time, however, one has to be selective. When it comes to Cathedral or Monastery Treasuries I have got to admit they are usually low on my list of priorities. However, I highly recommend this one - it is everything contrary to my previous experiences of Treasuries: it is well lit, spacious, thoughtfully laid out, beautifully presented and explained, displaying many fabulous, precious and exquisite items, the like of which you will never see close up again, and well worth marvelling over.

For some peace, quiet, thanksgiving and reflection, seek out the Adoration Chapel. It is located at choir loft level between the Basilica and the Chapel of Our Lady, it actually looks down into the nave of the Basilica below. It is a simple, plain, white-walled and vaulted room, with an effective and tasteful hint of exposed brick and stone work. Above the monstrance is the familiar picture of Jesus of the Divine Mercy, an original and a votive offering, from a local artist. The Blessed Sacrament is exposed during opening hours.

Unusual Stations of the Cross

One item that I would particularly like to draw to your attention is an extraordinarily powerful and expressive Stations of the Cross. I came across them quite accidentally and such was their impact that I actually stopped dead in my tracks and had to spend some time deciphering what they are all about.

They are the work of a contemporary Polish artist, Jerzy Duda Gracz, and consist of eighteen wall-sized paintings of the Stations - the last four depicting Resurrection, Doubting Thomas, Galilee and Ascension. They are graphic, detailed, deploying a very effective hint of caricature as a means of artistic emphasis. Jesus is shown as an ugly, skinny, vulnerable character with a long nose and straggly hair, but exuding suffering, pain, acquiescence, dignity and humility with every step to His

The Twelfth Station of the Cross as depicted by Jerzy Duda Gracz

Golgotha. He is surrounded by contemporary events, many reflecting the concentration camp and communist persecutions, and by contemporary people - both anonymous and recognisable. For instance, clearly evident at the dramatic Crucifixion scene, back-dropped by hundreds of crosses, is Pope John Paul II close by at the foot of the Cross with the icon of Our Lady of Częstochowa, and surrounded by the Saints, Kings, Queens, Bishops, Priests, Nuns of Polish history, including St Maximilian, St Faustina and Cardinal Wyszynski. These Stations are unflinching in their portrayal of Jesus' suffering, the suffering we inflict upon ourselves and each other, and our collective denial and wilful ignorance of that suffering.

In all, Jasna Góra is a thoroughly inspiring and interesting place to visit and at which to pray.

Auschwitz

Meditation

"To speak in this place of horror, in this place where unprecedented mass crimes were committed against God and man, is almost impossible - and it is particularly difficult and troubling for a Christian, for a Pope from Germany. In a place like this, words fail; in the end, there can only be a dread silence - a silence which is itself a heartfelt cry to God: Why, Lord, did you remain silent? How could you tolerate all this?
In silence, then, we bow our heads before the endless line of those who suffered and were put to death here; yet our silence becomes in turn a plea for forgiveness and reconciliation, a plea to the living God never to let this happen again".

(Pope Benedict XVI, on his visit to Auschwitz)

Auschwitz is a grim, disgusting place. But, for the sake of Pope Benedict's plea above, we must come here, with maturity and responsibility, to face up to and accept the horrors of this place at first-hand. "Why me?", you may ask, "It was nothing remotely to do with me". It is to a place like this that all generations should come, to witness at first hand how completely out of control humanity can become - something which we should not ignore or deny - in whichever generation it takes place. We need to come here to turn that silent plea for forgiveness and reconciliation into fervent and active prayer. We need to pray continuously, as we go round, for those countless tens of thousands of anguished, tortured souls who perished here, as well as for other victims in other such places of horror - and for those who still suffer - round the world, and throughout the whole of human history.

Oświęcim

When Poland was overrun by Germany in 1939, the small Polish town of Oświęcim and surrounding area was incorporated into the Third Reich, the town's name being changed to Auschwitz. A deserted pre-war Polish Army barracks on the outskirts of town was chosen as a most favourable location to build a concentration camp - a concept being developed to deal with the mass arrests, imprisonment and extermination of 'undesirables' to the Third Reich. In the chilling words of Heinrich Himmler, the architect of this mass murder, "The existing extermination centres in the East are not sufficient to cope with an operation on such a scale. Therefore I have designated Auschwitz for this purpose, both because of its convenient location as regards communication, and because the area can be easily isolated and camouflaged".

The camp came into being on 14th June 1940 with the despatch of 728 Polish political prisoners from Tarnow. Rudolf Hoess was appointed its first commandant. This camp, Auschwitz I - the so called 'Main Camp' - is quite compact, consisting principally of 28 red brick, one-storey barrack blocks, placed in neat, orderly rows. At its height it 'accommodated' up to 20,000 people in squalid, unsanitary conditions of gross overcrowding and misery. But belying these neat barrack blocks, and just outside the main fence of the camp, the squat ugly buildings of mass extermination - the first gas chamber and crematorium - unmistakable with its blunt, square chimney.

Auschwitz II and III

The pressure to house and process the increasing number of detainees became so intense as to require the building, by prisoner labour, of a much larger camp, some three kilometres away, at Birkenau (Brzezinka), as Auschwitz II. This camp was nine times larger than Auschwitz I, containing over 300 crude brick and wooden buildings, being divided into several separate camps to house differing groups of prisoners. At its peak the camp reached a total of over 100,000 inmates, all living and dying in appalling, inhuman circumstances of starvation, privation and violence. This camp was distinguished by its grim efficiency in mass elimination: it had four gas chambers and crematoria.

Auschwitz - entrance gate

The third element of the Auschwitz complex was established at nearby Monowice (Auschwitz III), on property owned by the German chemical plant IG-Farbenindustrie, to provide slave labour to this plant, as well as forty smaller outposts of Auschwitz III in nearby steelworks, mines and factories.

Unknown numbers

The exact figure of how many souls perished at Auschwitz will never be known, as in the latter years, a large proportion of Jews in the packed cattle wagons were taken straight from the unloading railhead at Birkenau to the adjacent gas chambers without any records or documentation. The best current historical estimate of the total of those who were killed varies from between 1.1 and 1.5 million people, with about 90 percent being Jews from all over Europe. A significant number of Polish Catholics (c150,000) were killed, as were Soviet PoWs, Roma and Sinti gypsies, and other minority 'undesirables'. Most died in the gas chambers, but others suffered excruciating deaths through starvation, disease, over-work, brutality, executions, and some from the effects of the sinister medical experiments carried out at Auschwitz I by Josef Mengele, known as the 'Angel of Death'.

When the Soviet army liberated Auschwitz on 27th January 1945, only 7,600 emaciated, abandoned prisoners greeted them with blank and apathetic disbelief; they were the fortunate ones - some 58,000 had been forcibly marched away from the Soviet advance into Germany, most of whom perished on this 'death march'.

In 1947 the Polish government established the former Auschwitz-Birkenau Concentration camps as a State Museum as 'a warning for generations to come'. It is a UNESCO World Heritage site, having been visited by 25,000,000 people since opening, and now by some 700,000 a year, many of whom are groups of young people. In 1979 the newly elected Pope John Paul II celebrated Mass there for some 500,000 people, and Benedict XVI visited on 28th May 2006.

Auschwitz I

If arriving by train at Oświęcim, the site is about twenty minutes' walk, or a short bus ride, from the station. It is well organised, well laid out and signed. There are very adequate self-guide booklets, well marked routes and self explanatory displays for those who may wish to proceed at their own pace, and contemplate events here more deeply and thoughtfully. Expert guides are available, though. An introductory film is screened in the Reception building, with English showings at specified times - it is sombre viewing, but worth watching.

As you come out of the Information and Reception block you head down a wide, cobbled path towards the infamous entry gate to the camp, over which is the ironic motto *Arbeit Macht Frei* (Work will set you Free), then passing by the SS Guardhouse and watch tower on the left as you go through. Just through the main gate, on the right, an illustration showing where the camp orchestra played their tunes of grisly false jollity as prisoners were mustered or marched to work at the beginning of each day. Just pause now before you go any further…

> "The most important prayer at the threshold
> of Auschwitz is - Silence:
> Silence
> Listening
> Searching
> the voice of Auschwitz
> the voice of your own heart
> the voice of the other
> the voice of God"
> (Centre of Dialogue and Peace)

Grim displays

"The one who does not remember history is bound to live through it again."
(George Santayana)

The different displays are set up in the redbrick barrack blocks, of which, above the doorway of one, is etched the stark reality of the philosopher Santayana's sentiment.

Each block depicts in unflinching and unsparing detail the whole process of the 'extermination factory'. Starting from who was brought here, from where, and in what numbers, and how. What fate awaited them on arrival - execution for those not fit to work, separation of women from men, those singled out for hard labour or medical experimentation. Then the photographs of individuals - hundreds of them, lining many of the blocks' corridor and room walls - blank, uncomprehending, wooden stares at the impersonal camera lens; the occasional glare of defiance; occasionally and bizarrely, even the hint of a smile, in what can only have been an automatic response from those who may have been used to smiling at a pointed camera in happier times.

Technical drawings are shown, down to the last detail; models of the gas chambers and crematoria are on display, all illustrating in a ghastly impersonal and objective engineering manner, the mechanics of mass extermination. Then the heartbreaking displays of all the human effects from this industrialised process: a bank of hair shorn from arriving prisoners, lining one side of a sizeable room behind a sloping glass display cabinet; piles of children's shoes; heaps of spectacles; a large collection of false limbs and prosthetics, looking bizarre and forlorn having been permanently separated from their crippled owners; shaving and washing items - in fact, every item of personal existence brought by those hopeful people who had been told were going to a new life of resettlement, is on display. It was all re-used - being sorted, packed up and redistributed in Germany, in a huge operation of a macabre recycling scheme.

The children

The most poignant for me was the higgledy-piggeldy display of piled suitcases, all named and designated by their owners in the optimistic hope of being reunited with them on arrival, unpacking and getting settled in to a new life - the reality was their plunder. One random suitcase caught my eye - with *Maria Kafka* boldly declaring her ownership on it: who were you Marie, what did you look like, where did you come from, how old were you, were you alone, how and when did you die? All questions that can be asked a million times…with very few, if any, answers.

And then the displays showing routines at the camp - work details, living conditions, feeding arrangements - some shown by artists' pictures and drawings who suffered there. In one of the rooms there is a heartbreaking exhibition about the children who were sent here: photographs, belongings, clothes - emaciated, starving, suffering, bewildered children.

> ### *Prayer*
>
> "God of Our Fathers, let the ashes of the children incinerated in Auschwitz, the rivers of blood spilled at Babi Yar or Majdanek, be a warning to mankind that hatred is destructive, violence is contagious, while man has an unlimited capacity to cruelty. Almighty God, fulfil the prophecy of Isaiah: "They shall beat their swords into ploughshares...nation shall not lift up a sword against nation, neither shall they learn war any more". Amen.
>
> (Alexander Kimel, a Holocaust survivor)

Block 11

You then come to Blocks 10 and 11, in the top right hand corner of the camp. Block 10 was where the medical experimentation was carried out. Block 11 was the grim punishment and execution block - the ground floor and cellars being retained in their original form. It is here, in the cellars, that you can view the dark, claustrophobic cell where St Maximilian Kolbe endured his last days, comforting his fellow prisoners who were sentenced to death by starvation. Father Kolbe, the last survivor of this group, in the end had to be killed by lethal injection (see CTS booklet *Maximilian Kolbe*). There are various displays upstairs, amongst which a section on St Maximilian. There you will see a copy of his Death

Certificate - as neat a bit of bureaucracy as you will see anywhere, attempting to offer legitimacy to murder - primly signed and stamped, duly recording that he died on 14th August 1941 precisely at 12:50pm...no cause of death appears to be given.

In between Blocks 10 and 11 is the enclosed courtyard where the grim Execution Wall stands, against which countless victims were lined up and summarily shot; it was also the area where unspeakable brutality and torture was inflicted - hence the blind shutters of Block 10 overlooking the yard, so that it could not be observed. In this area you may wish to join in meditation and prayer with St Maximilian Kolbe...

Meditation

Every man and woman in this world has been assigned a mission by God. In fact, ever since God created the universe, he arranged the first causes in such a way that the unbroken chain of their effects should create the most favourable conditions and circumstances for each person to fulfil the mission that God has assigned him.

Therefore, every person is born with abilities that are proportionate to the mission he or she has been entrusted, and throughout each person's whole life, the environment, circumstances, and everything else will contribute to make it easy and possible for him or her to reach that purpose.

In fact, each person's perfection consists in reaching that purpose; and the more thoroughly one's task is carried out, and the more scrupulously one's mission is fulfilled, the greater and holier he or she shall be before the eyes of God. Besides natural gifts, every person is also accompanied by the grace of God from the cradle to the tomb. God's grace is poured on each of us in such quantity and quality that our weak human nature strengthens itself by acquiring the supernatural energy we need to face our own mission.

(St Maximillian Kolbe)

Crematorium

Your intense pilgrimage in this area is coming to an end as you pass back down through the barrack blocks - many given over to displaying individual country's aspects to this memorial site. On your way through you will notice all the small, incongruous details - the rather smart, enlarged, Tyrolean-looking sentry box in which the mustering officials took shelter in inclement weather, the crude gallows from which collective hangings were made, the pleasant green trees, the warm, innocuous brickwork.

And then finally, through the gas chamber and crematorium of Auschwitz I. An ugly, sinister, foreboding place, in which one does not linger…just noting the stark bare concrete walls, floor and ceiling - the last view for those who perished; and then the furnace trolleys, extended out of their furnaces on their miniature rails…having made their final short journey those many, many years ago…we may pause here and pray…

> ***Prayer***
>
> "Dear Lord Jesus, despite what we see and feel and know what happened at this place of dread - unspeakable mass crimes are still being perpetrated against humanity and against God. Please help us to have some bearing against this most abhorrent abuse of Your most precious gift - our free will. For it is all in *our* hands that these things happen. You show us quite unequivocally the Way, the Truth and the Life.
>
> Despite the futility and helplessness that we may feel as individuals as to how we may effectively cast Your influence against evil, let us commit ourselves in Faith and Trust into *Your* hands, and show those around us, by the example of Love, that we are prepared to witness to the Truth and attempt sincerely to live the Life.
>
> We can only believe and hope and trust in your Divine Plan that the Victory is Yours, outside time and for all Eternity, for all those souls who seek and desire Your Mercy. Amen".

It is nothing but with relief that one emerges from this place, but noting nearby, the gallows from where Rudolf Hoess, the commandant was hanged on 16th April 1947.

There is no sensationalism or over-dramatisation in portraying what went on here. It is factually and soberly presented, and well displayed. All of those going round the site did so in stunned silence - sombre, grim-faced, and disbelieving. Even the groups of normally exuberant young people were passive and subdued.

Meditation

In speaking of the victims of Auschwitz, I cannot fail to recall that, in the midst of that unspeakable concentration of evil, there were also heroic examples of commitment to good. Certainly there were many persons who were willing, in spiritual freedom, to endure suffering and to show love, not only for their fellow prisoners, but also for their tormentors. Many did so out of love for God and for man; others in the name of the highest spiritual values. Their attitude bore clear witness to a truth which is often expressed in the Bible: even though man is capable of evil, and at times boundless evil, evil itself will never have the last word. In the very abyss of suffering, love can triumph. The witness to this love shown in Auschwitz must never be forgotten. It must never cease to rouse consciences, to resolve conflicts, to inspire the building of peace.

(Pope John Paul II)

Birkenau

This is not the end of it, though. I would very strongly recommend going on to Birkenau as part of your pilgrimage here. Buses run regularly to and fro, taxis are also available.

In many ways Birkenau is a complete contrast to the forced intimacy of Aushwitz I - it is vast. Almost as far as the eye can see, on an immense, flat area of 171 hectares, is the wire and compounds, the standing and ruined huts, the railway, and of course the famous arch through which the cattle wagons with their human cargo passed before offloading. Here, you feel more alone, because of the emptiness of the place. There is plenty to look at and ponder over.

One can wander at will, peering into the crude, low, red-brick prison huts with their three-tiered continuous pallets, into which were crammed those attempting to sleep. In the Women's Camp (Compound B1a) have a peep into Hut 13 (16) where you will see two large crude children's original drawings on a wall, portraying what must have been to them a fairy story of long forgotten times past - that of children happily taking themselves off to school - heart rending.

The larger, wooden buildings were originally stables, which became, with the installed tiers of pallet beds, instant accommodation for about 1,000 souls in each, in the most awful conditions.

It was here that Edith Stein - St Teresa Benedicta of the Cross - a Jewish convert, eminent philosopher and Carmelite nun, was murdered, with her sister Rosa, also a Carmelite, on about the 9th of August 1942 (see CTS booklets *Edith Stein,* and *Europe's soul and her Patron Saints*).

"Whoever belongs to Christ, must go the whole way with Him. He must mature to adulthood: he must one day or other walk the way of the cross to Gethsemane and Golgotha."
(St Teresa Benedicta of the Cross)

Victims' Monument

Right up at the top end of the camp, beyond the end of the railway siding, are the gruesome four crematoria, in ruins, but certainly decipherable as to their construct and intent. By crematoria II and III is set the International Monument to the Victims of Fascism, a large, ugly, abstract jumble of ill-fitting and blackened, roughened concrete shapes, of which, no matter how hard I tried, I could make no sense - but perhaps that is its purpose. At the foot of this memorial, in every European language, are large, bronze plaques which read:

"For ever let this place be a cry of despair, and a warning to Humanity, where the Nazis murdered about one and a half million men, women and children, mainly Jews from various countries of Europe. Auschwitz-Birkenau 1940-1945".

Sometimes, in places like this - and I think particularly of the Commonwealth War Graves - amongst the mass destruction of yesteryear, one can feel a sense of peace. But here, despite a benign, sunny early summer day, pleasant greenery, blue sky, solitude and quiet, there was absolutely no feeling of peace whatsoever - only anguish and hopelessness, and even anger. But let us spend some time here, close to the Monument, close to the sinister crematoria, close to those dark ponds of human ashes, close to a dark period of history, and cast our loving prayers of light over all who perished.

"The words of our prayers are different, but our tears are the same."

(Abraham Joshua Heschel)

Meditation:
KADDISH - Jewish prayer for the dead

*"May the Great Name whose desire gave birth
to the Universe resound through the Creation now.*

*May this Great Presence rule your life and
your day and all lives of our World.
And say, Yes. Amen.*

*Throughout all Space, Bless, Bless this Great Name,
Throughout all Time.
Though we bless, we praise, we beautify,*

We offer up your Name,
Name That Is Holy, Blessed One,
Still you remain beyond the reach of our praise, our song,
Beyond the reach of all consolation. Beyond! Beyond!
And say, Yes. Amen.

Let God's Name give birth to Great Peace and Life
For us and all people
And say, Yes. Amen.

The One who has given a universe of Peace
Gives peace to us, to All that is Israel.
And say, Yes. Amen."

At the close of Pope Benedict's visit, when he was at the Monument, the prevailing rain and grey clouds parted, and through which a rainbow brightly shone. "It was a source of great comfort to me at that moment to see a rainbow appearing in the sky as, before the horrors of that place, I cried out to God like Job, shaken by the dread of his apparent absence but at the same time supported by the certainty that even in his silence he does not cease to be and remain with us. The rainbow was, as it were, a response: *Yes, I exist, and the words of the promise, of the Covenant which I spoke after the flood, are still valid today.*"

And so he concluded his visit: "At Auschwitz-Birkenau humanity walked through a "valley of darkness".

And so, here in this place, I would like to end with a prayer of trust - with one of the Psalms of Israel which is also a prayer of Christians:

The Lord is my shepherd, I shall not want. He makes me lie down in green pastures; he leads me beside still waters; he restores my soul. He leads me in right paths for his name's sake. Even though I walk through the valley of the shadow of death, I fear no evil; for you are with me; your rod and your staff - they comfort me...I shall dwell in the house of the Lord my whole life long. (Ps 23:1-4,6)

"But the souls of the upright are in the hands of God,
And no torment can touch them.
To the unenlightened they appeared to die,
Their departure was regarded as a disaster,
Their leaving us like annihilation;
But they are at peace." (Ws 3:1,2)

Centre for Information, Meetings, Dialogue, Education and Prayer: Close to the former concentration camp, this is a Catholic institution founded in 1992 in co-operation with Jewish representatives. The aim of the Centre is to create a place for reflection, education, sharing and prayer for all those who are moved by what happened here. It runs formal retreat programmes, and visiting groups are advised to contact the Centre ahead of their visit so that their needs can be catered for. Casual visitors are welcome; there is a chapel, restaurant and exhibits. Further details can be seen at: *http://www.centrum-dialogu.oświęcim.pl/*

The Carmelite convent at Karmelitanki Bose ul. Legionów 92a 32-600 Oświęcim. This is also nearby. Check with the Centre above as to the availability of the convent chapel for prayer or Mass times.

The Parish of the Franciscan Friars run a guest house, about 5km from Auschwitz at Harmęże: Klasztor Franciszkanów Harmęże, ul. Franciszkańska 12 32-600 Oświęcim. *http://www.harmeze.franciszkanie.pl/*

Mercy and Reconciliation

As I had rather vaguely hoped before I set off, my pilgrimage to Poland did reveal with clarity that indefinable connection between the human brutality of Auschwitz and the Divine Mercy of God. It came from a completely unexpected and unsolicited direction - through a Polish priest that I met at the Divine Mercy Shrine in Kraków. I was explaining to him why I was in Poland, and saying how I was dreading going to Auschwitz the next day. After some generalities about the place, he then said, "My great uncle, a Jesuit Provincial, heard the confession of Rudolf Hoess (the Commandant of Auschwitz) before he went to his execution." This of course rocked me back, and I could only think of asking, "Did your uncle think it a 'good' confession?" "He must have done", was the reply, "because he took Holy Communion to him the next day."

My initial reaction was of shock, that seemingly, this one simple, relatively swift act would absolve Hoess of his grotesque, long term and extreme crimes against humanity. "Would I be surprised if I saw Hoess in heaven?" I asked. "No, don't be surprised, and of course, it is only God that knows what was in that man's heart, but if Hoess was genuinely repentant, he would be forgiven, no matter how grave his sin." Sensing my extreme unease at this prospect, he added, "My uncle's thought about Hoess' Purgatory is that he would have to look each and every one of his victims in the eye and convince them of his remorse." This somehow put some context against the requirement for reparation, but of course, that aspect is only that priest's human, 'unofficial' viewpoint, and my own 'take' on it entirely human as well.

The implications of this are of course enormous, and to discuss them all fully in a book such as this would not be possible. Apart from contradicting history - which judges Hoess as going to his death unapologetic for his crimes - it does pose this question of forgiveness - given the enormity of scale. It should also be noted that Hoess was brought up in a strict Roman Catholic family, so he would not be unaware of the Sacrament of Reconciliation, and what it stands for.

God will forgive, but how hard - impossible - for those who suffered so dreadfully, to offer forgiveness? I have heard of instances of emotional and heartfelt 'second generation' forgiveness. One particular one that stands out in my mind was at the Shrine of Divine Mercy, between a Polish bishop and a German lady, both whose parents were at Auschwitz respectively as victim and perpetrator.

I can only set all this in the context of what God tells us about His Divine Mercy - and personally attempt to work from there.

Jesus, speaking to Saint Faustina: "Write, speak of My mercy. Tell souls where they are to look for solace; that is, in the Tribunal of Mercy [*the Sacrament of Reconciliation*]. There the greatest of miracles take place [*and*] are incessantly repeated. To avail oneself of this miracle, it is not necessary to go on a great pilgrimage or to carry out some external ceremony; it suffices to come with faith to the feet of My representative and to reveal to him one's misery, and the miracle of Divine Mercy will be fully demonstrated. Were a soul like a decaying corpse so that from a human standpoint, there would be no [*hope of*] restoration and everything would be lost, it is not so with God. The miracle of Divine Mercy restores that soul in full. Oh, how miserable are those who do not take advantage of the miracle of God's mercy! You will call out in vain, but it will be too late."

The Catechism: "There is no offence, however serious, that the Church cannot forgive. 'There is no-one, however wicked and guilty, who may not confidently hope for forgiveness, provided his repentance is honest.' Christ who died for all men desires that in His Church the gates of forgiveness should always be open to anyone who turns away from sin." (*CCC* 982)

The assurances of God's Mercy to us and the world abound in the Old and New Testaments. At the simplest level we assert this every time we say the Lord's Prayer: "...forgive us our trespasses...", but just as significantly we pray, "…as we forgive those who trespass against us…" In this last aspect, Jesus makes it quite clear, when Peter asked him, "'Lord, how often must I forgive my brother if he wrongs me? As often as seven times?' Jesus answered, 'Not seven, I tell you, but seventy seven times.'" (*Mt* 18:21-22)

"Yet you are merciful to all, because you are almighty, You overlook people's sins, so that they can repent."
(*Ws* 11:22)

Bibliography

Catechism of the Catholic Church, Geoffrey Chapman, London, 1999.

The Rough Guide to Poland, Jonathan Bousfield and Mark Slater, Rough Guides, London, New York, Delhi, 2005.

Saint of Auschwitz, The Story of Maksymilian Kolbe, Diana Dewar, Darton, Longman and Todd, London, 1982.

Diary of St Maria Faustina Kowalska, Marian Press, Stockbridge, MA, 2007.

Memory and Identity, John Paul II, Weidenfield and Nicolson, London, 2005.

Auschwitz, the Nazis and the Final Solution, Lawrence Rees, BBC Books, London, 2005.

Edith Stein Essential Writings, John Sullivan OCD, Orbis Books, New York, 2005.

Eye Witness Travel - Cracow, Ewa Szwagrzyk (Managing Editor), Dorling Kindersley Ltd, London, 2007.

CTS

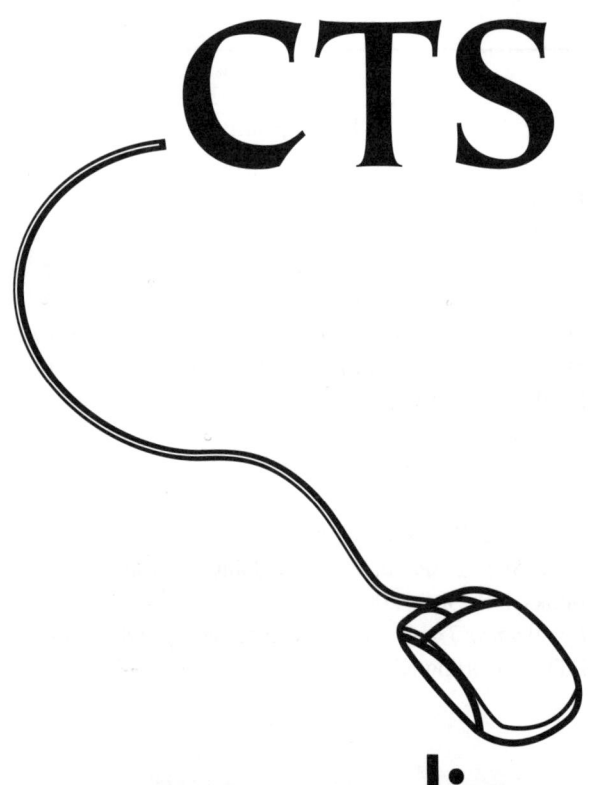

... now online
www.cts-online.org.uk

Rome -
A Pilgrim's Companion

Rome - the Eternal City! But where should a visitor begin to explore it? This pilgrim's companion takes you on several carefully planned routes, to discover with wonder and prayer the heart of Rome and of the Catholic world. Bursting with history and beauty, Rome's architectural wonders are outmatched only by the rich spiritual legacy of its saints and martyrs. Meditations and prayers punctuate each route, and there is a thorough index of people and places in support.

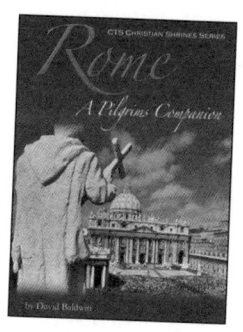

ISBN: 1 86082 325 4
CTS Code: D 676

Informative Catholic Reading

We hope that you have enjoyed reading this booklet.

If you would like to find out more about CTS booklets - we'll send you our free information pack and catalogue.

Please send us your details:

Name ....

Address ....

....

....

Postcode ....

Telephone ....

Email ....

Send to: CTS, 40-46 Harleyford Road,
          Vauxhall, London
          SE11 5AY

Tel: 020 7640 0042
Fax: 020 7640 0046
Email: info@cts-online.org.uk